CARTOON NETWORK SCOOBY-DOO!

Phonics Reading Program

BOOK 2: short e, o, u

Shaggy's Nice, Hot Breakfast

by Frances Ann Ladd

Illustrated by Duendes del Sur

SCHOLASTIC INC.

New York Toronto London Auckland Sydney
Mexico City New Delhi Hong Kong Buenos Aires

Shaggy got up
out of bed.
He was hungry.
"The clock says
breakfast!"
said Shaggy.
"My tummy says
hot dog!"

"I bet I know what you want, buddy." Scooby begged for Scooby Snacks.

HOT DOG
HOT DOGS

They went to the
hot dog truck.
Shaggy stepped up
to tell the man
what they wanted
to get.

"Let me get
a hot dog, please.
Lots and lots
of hot dogs."

Shaggy got a hot dog.
"Just my luck.
The bun is crusty.
Oh, well."
Shaggy took a bite.

"Help!" Shaggy yelled.
Then he hopped up
and down.
"Hot, hot dog!
Hot, hot dog!"

SD

The hot dogs cooled.
Shaggy ate lots
of hot dogs.
Then he patted
his tummy.
"Well, that was fun,"
he said.

"What's for lunch?"
asked Shaggy.